Real LOVE COMPANION

Taking steps toward a loving and happy life.

GREG BAER, M.D.

BLUE RIDGE PRESS
©2006. All rights reserved.

The Real Love® Companion—Taking Steps Toward a Loving and Happy Life

Copyright © 2012 by Greg Baer, M.D.

Second Edition

All rights reserved including the right of reproduction in whole or in part in any form.

Baer, Greg
    The Real Love Companion
    ISBN 1-892319-12-8
    Non Fiction
Published by Blue Ridge Press PO Box 3075 Rome, GA 30164
    877-633-3568

Also by Greg Baer, M.D.—

Published by Gotham Books, a division of Penguin USA Group:

Real Love® — The Truth About Finding Unconditional Love and Fulfilling Relationships

Real Love® *in Marriage* — The Truth About Finding Genuine Happiness Now and Forever

Published by Blue Ridge Press:

Real Love® — The Truth About Finding Unconditional Love and Fulfilling Relationships, Unabridged Audio Book — Seven 60 minute CDs

Real Love® *for Wise Men and Women* — The Truth About Sharing Real Love

Real Love® *in Dating* — The Truth About Finding the Perfect Partner — Book and Unabridged Audio Book

Real Love® *in Marriage* — Unabridged Audio Book, Blue Ridge Press

40 Days to Real Love® *and Happiness in Your Marriage* — A Companion Workbook for Real Love in Marriage

Real Love® *in Parenting* — The Truth About Raising Happy and Responsible Children — Book and Unabridged Audio Book

Real Love® *and Freedom for the Soul* — Eliminating the Chains of Victimhood

Real Love® *in the Workplace* — Eight Principles for Consistently Effective Leadership in Business

Real Love® *and Post-Childhood Stress Disorder* — Treating Your Unrecognized Post Traumatic Stress Disorder

The Truth About Love and Lies — Three 60 minute CDs

The Essentials of Real Love® — Six DVDs, or Six CDs

The Essentials of Real Love® *Workbook* for DVDs or CDs

The Essentials of Real Love® *Bible Workbook* for DVDs or CDs

Under the Bridge — a novel

Printed in the United States

10 9 8 7 6 5 4 3 2 1

The Real Love Companion

Taking Steps Toward a Loving and Happy Life

The principles in the book, *Real Love*, have proven to be life-changing for thousands of people across the country. Simply reading the book, however, is not enough. As we read, we must see how the individual principles apply to *us*, and we must be motivated to tell the truth about ourselves to create opportunities for people to unconditionally accept and love us.

Books don't change people. Real Love does, and it is the purpose of this Companion to help us *experience* Real Love in our lives.

Throughout the Companion, I will make suggestions about what you might do to apply the principles of Real Love to yourself. On each occasion when I make a suggestion to think about a principle, or discuss an incident or insight, you can do one or more of the following:

1. You can answer the question or do the exercise by yourself, as a means of more closely examining your own life and taking more productive action. You might write down the answers to the questions and read them later. This workbook is printed on one side of the page so you might use the blank side to make notes as you read.

2. You can read the *Companion* with a friend. As you answer the questions with a friend, you will create the life-giving opportunities to feel accepted and loved by another person.

3. You can use the *Companion* in a group meeting, the kind briefly mentioned on pp. 94-5 of *Real Love*. As group meetings first begin, people often have difficulty knowing how to start telling the truth about themselves. This Companion will get them started in that process in a way that doesn't require as much creativity and initial discomfort on their part. For much more information and guidance about group meetings, see *The Wise Man—The Truth About Sharing Real Love*, available on the website at www.RealLove.com.

Each section of the *Companion* will address specified pages in *Real Love*, and I'll assume you're familiar with the contents of those pages. On the whole I won't summarize what is found in *Real Love*.

INTRODUCTION

On pp. xi-xiii, I describe how I felt empty and alone despite all my experiences with "success." What experiences have you had with success, and have you felt a similar emptiness and disappointment after all the work you put into achieving it?

Notes

CHAPTER ONE

The Missing Ingredient: What Relationships Really Need

Pp. 1-2. Blaming Others

Describe some times when you've blamed other people for the anger or disappointment you've felt, as Lisa blamed Doug for the unhappiness she felt in their marriage. For example:

- I was angry at the boss because he blamed me for something I didn't do, and because he didn't appreciate what I did.

- I was angry at my husband because he didn't do something he'd promised.

- I was angry at my wife because she was late.

- I got angry at the kids when they didn't go to bed on time.

Talk about these experiences with a friend or in a group meeting.

Pp. 6-7. Visualization

Discuss what it was like for you as you did the visualization on these pages.

- Could you picture what it would be like to feel unconditionally loved like that?

- During the time you were with those people, did you have an any inclination to feel angry at those people, or lie to them, or withdraw from them?

- During the time you were with the people who unconditionally loved you, did you feel any inclination to feel angry at *anyone*, even those out in the real world?

- What would you give to be able to feel like that all the time?

As you learn the principles in *Real Love* and in the *Real Love Companion*, and as you apply them to your life, you will find the love you imagined in the visualization.

Pp. 8-9. Identifying Real Love vs. Imitation Love

Imagine someone in your life who you want to love unconditionally, and then imagine that you actually feel unconditionally loving toward that person. You care about his or her happiness more than anything in the world. Imagine describing to him a mistake he's made. Caring primarily about *his* happiness, would you be angry as you described the mistake, or would you calmly talk about the mistake for *his* benefit—simply so he could avoid the mistake and be happier?

Now describe the last time you were angry at someone for making a mistake that inconvenienced you. Can you see how your disappointment and anger were *not* for the benefit of the other person? Can you see how your anger is always selfish? Discuss this with a friend or a group.

Notes

Pp. 9-12. The Effect of Lacking Real Love

Describe people in your life who have been disappointed and angry at you when you didn't behave in a way they wanted: parents, teachers, spouse, peers, and so on. On those occasions, do you see how their love for you was conditional? Do you see how hurtful that was to you, to know that you had to perform at a certain level to be considered worthwhile and lovable?

Discuss the possibility that your own parents did not sufficiently love you unconditionally. This is an important realization, because that lack of Real Love from early in life is why you have difficulty in your marriage, with your children, and in your job. Your frustration and anger with anyone in the present is always founded on a profound unhappiness that began with insufficient Real Love in childhood. It will be easier to talk about this if you also realize that your parents loved you *as well as they could*. But anything other than Real Love is never enough. Parents have a huge responsibility for the unhappiness in our lives, and we need to talk about it—not to blame them, or to make excuses for how we feel and what we do now, but only to *recognize* the effect that lack of Real Love has had on us. We also must realize that changing our lives is now entirely *our* responsibility.

Pp. 15-17. Drowning

Think of someone in your life who is hurting you with his or her lies, anger, or withdrawal. Now imagine that this person is behaving badly not to hurt you but only because she's drowning in the absence of Real Love. Can you stay angry at someone who is drowning? Imagine how your feelings will change toward this person as you realize that you and she just need more Real Love in your lives.

CHAPTER TWO

Getting and Protecting: The Many Faces of Imitation Love

Pp. 18-21. Imitation Love

Describe how you use praise as a form of Imitation Love:

- Do you enjoy people seeing you as sexually desirable, and do you devote considerable time and effort to enhancing your appearance?

- Do you get a real sense of worth from your accomplishments in school and at work? When you're having problems at school or work, does that negatively affect how you feel about yourself?

- Do you draw attention to the good things you do so people will flatter you?

- Do you get a sense of importance and accomplishment when people are grateful to you for the things you do for them? Are you disappointed when people are *not* grateful for the things you do?

- Do you like it when people know how much money you make?

Notes

Describe how you use power as a form of Imitation Love:

- Do you often correct your husband or wife when he or she speaks?

- Do you control the behavior of your children on occasions when it might be better to let them make their own decisions?

- Do you persuade people to your point of view?

- Do you often insist on being right in an argument?

- Do you like to dominate conversations?

- Do you enjoy telling your employees what to do?

- Do you use sex to get men to do what you want?

Describe how you use pleasure as a form of Imitation Love:

- Do you enjoy looking at women and fantasizing about having sex with them?

- Do you enjoy driving very fast?

- Do you eat more than you should?

- Do you watch video games for hours when you know you could be doing a lot better things with your time?

Describe how you use safety as a form of Imitation Love:

- Do you avoid situations where you could look foolish?

- Do you say you have a "good" relationship with your husband, when the truth is, you've just learned not to push

Notes

each other's buttons? Do you feel genuinely loved, or do you just feel relatively safe and comfortable?

- Are you qualified for a much better job but stay in the same one because you can't stand the thought of going out there and being rejected?

- Do you leave relationships when they get difficult?

Pp. 22-3. The Effects of Imitation Love

Describe how you've seen the effect of Imitation Love—one or more of those you talked about above—wear off after a time, causing you to seek more and more of it, but never finding real satisfaction.

Pp. 24-7. Getting and Protecting Behaviors

Describe how you use lying as a Getting and Protecting Behavior:

- Do you often make excuses for your mistakes?

- Do you let other people do what they want, because if you don't, you're afraid they won't like you?

- Do you love to talk about your accomplishments but avoid talking about your mistakes, flaws, and fears?

- Do you often say what other people want to hear?

- Do you sometimes flatter people so they'll like you?

We use attacking as a Getting and Protecting Behavior so often and with such subtlety, we often fail to recognize that we're doing it:

- When people don't do what you want, do you often become angry? And have you noticed that when you become angry, people sometimes give in and do what you want?

Notes

- When you get angry, have you noticed that your children tend to move faster and do what you want?

- When people don't do what you want, do you sometimes make them feel guilty and motivate them to change their mind?

- When someone gets angry at you, do you sometimes get them to back down from attacking you by getting even angrier at them and intimidating them?

Describe how you act like a victim:

- Do you sometimes get sympathy from people by drawing attention to what someone has done to you?

- Do you often complain about how things are just not "fair?"

- When you make mistakes, do you often say, "It's not my fault," or "I couldn't help it?"

- Do you often talk about what people should have done for you?

Describe how you run to protect yourself:

- Do you claim to be shy?

- When a conversation is difficult, do you tend to withdraw and become quiet?

- When you get irritated, do you sulk?

- Do you sometimes have a drink or two after work, just to take the edge off the tension?

Notes

Describe how you cling to get Imitation Love:

- Do you ask your adult children why they haven't called you in a long time?

- Do you sometimes give people gifts so they'll feel grateful or obligated to you in some way? Before you think to say *no*, ask how you'd feel if people were completely *ungrateful* for the gifts you gave.

- When your husband goes somewhere for the evening, do you ever say, "Do you have to go out tonight? We never do anything together."

- When someone is ending a relationship with you, do you tell them how much they'll be hurting you by leaving?

Pp. 27-9. The Effects of Getting and Protecting Behaviors

As you talk about some of the Getting and Protecting Behaviors you have used, honestly describe the rewards you've gotten from them:

- When I get angry, I feel less empty and afraid temporarily, but I never feel closer to people or genuinely happy.

- When I lie to people, I can often get out of trouble—I can even get people to accept me for a moment—but my lies isolate me. I never feel loved unconditionally while I'm lying.

- When I act like a victim, I like the sympathy I get, but I get tired of manipulating people, and eventually they get tired of my complaining.

- I've run from people and situations all my life. It makes me feel safer, but then I always feel alone.

Notes

- I can see that I've used Getting and Protecting Behaviors all my life, but they've never gotten me the kind of happiness I want.

P. 33-7. Using Getting and Protecting Behaviors and Imitation Love

Describe an incident—perhaps like that of Frank and Diane—where you used Getting and Protecting Behaviors to establish a relationship, where you exchanged Imitation Love and thought you were happy, and then discovered that your relationship was not based on Real Love.

CHAPTER THREE

Being Seen and Getting Loved:
The Tale of the Wart King and the Wise Man

Pp. 41-4. The Wart King

Can you see any similarities between you and the Wart King? Are you willing to do what he did to find the Real Love he found from the Wise Man?

Pp. 44-7. The Effect of Getting and Protecting Behaviors

Describe how you have manipulated people with Getting Behaviors to give you the acceptance and attention you've wanted. As in the story of the apples, can you see how your manipulations have instantly made it impossible for you to feel Real Love, no matter how much Imitation Love you get temporarily?

P. 47. Identifying Real Love

Considering the criteria on this page for identifying Real Love, how consistently have you received Real Love from other people? How consistently have you *given* Real Love to others?

Pp. 48-9. Relationships

Describe how you have tried to make a relationship (or relationships) what you *wanted*, rather than accepting it as the natural result of

the independent choices made by you and your partner. When have you tried to blend blue and yellow and expected to make orange?

Pp. 49-58. Changing Our Partners

Have you ever tried to change a partner to be more convenient for you, as Joan did with Tyler? Describe how your efforts turned out. Did your manipulations make you feel closer to that person? Did you feel more unconditionally loved? Genuinely happier?

Pp. 52-5. Disappointment, Anger, and Expectations

Think of someone toward whom you have felt disappointment or irritation lately. Can you see that those feelings result from your expectations that that person will behave in a way convenient for you? Can you see how expectations are a way you use to control people, and that they cause disappointment and anger? Are you willing to begin letting go of your expectations, so you can experience the unconditional love and happiness you really want?

Pp. 58-60. The Three Choices

Identify a relationship or situation where you're feeling irritated and frustrated. Describe how you are making the angry and foolish choice—to live with it and hate it—or the non-choice, to control the behavior of another person. Consider the wisdom of making a different choice: to learn to be accepting and loving—live with it and like it—or to leave it.

Describe what you'd have to do to make the loving choice.

CHAPTER FOUR

Taking the Leap of Faith:
Everyday Wise Men and How to Find Them

Pp. 65-7. The Desire to Change

Are you satisfied with your life exactly as it is, or would you like it to be much, much more? Would you like to eliminate the anger and frustration and replace them with love and joy?

Identify a situation or relationship you're not happy with. Are you willing to admit that you are wrong? To be sure, the other people involved have made their own mistakes, but are you willing to identify where *you* haven't been sufficiently loving?

Pp. 68-80. Faith

You've had a lifetime to prove beyond doubt that Imitation Love and all the Getting and Protecting Behaviors can't bring you Real Love or genuine happiness. Are you willing to exercise the faith required to start telling the truth about yourself and create the possibility that you can find Real Love?

People use Getting and Protecting Behaviors only as a reaction to their emptiness and fear. Are you willing to accept that? If so, you'll have faith that people are doing the best they can to love you, and that they are only behaving badly because they're drowning and trying to keep their heads above water. With that faith, you'll lose your anger at other people when they don't behave as you'd like.

Notes

Pp. 80-96. Telling the Truth about Yourself

Think of a recent experience where you made an excuse for a mistake you made, or you told a partial truth, or you outright lied to cover up your mistake. Now tell the whole truth about that mistake, taking complete responsible for what you did. At the very least write it down, but even better, tell a friend or group of friends. Then watch the face of the person you're telling and realize that you're being accepted while you're telling the truth about a mistake.

Pp. 87-9. More Truth-Telling

Describe a recent interaction that went badly. Describe how *you* were wrong in that interaction. It's irrelevant what the other person did. Talk only about *your* demands, *your* expectations, your anger, your other Getting and Protecting Behaviors, and your selfishness. Talk to people about this until you find someone who understands that you were wrong and accepts you *with* your warts.

Pp. 92-3. Talking about the Book, *Real Love*

Choose a friend or family member who you think you might be able to share the truth with. Make a commitment to talk to them about what you're learning about Real Love. It might be easier if you simply gave that person a copy of the book and asked them if they'd like to read about some things you've been learning lately.

Pp. 96-103. The Rules of Seeing

Talk about a recent interaction where you violated the First or Second Rules of seeing, and discuss how your behavior led to an unproductive conversation.

Write down some things people have said to you that have resulted in your feeling hurt or irritated. Now apply the Third Rule of Seeing, and translate what they said into what they were really saying about themselves. For example:

What Was Said to You	What the Speaker was Saying About Him(her)self
"You're always late."	"When you make me wait, I feel like you're telling me you don't care about me, and then I feel empty, helpless, and afraid."
"We never have sex."	"My life is already pretty empty, and then when you don't want to have sex with me, I feel even more unloved and alone."
"What's wrong with you?"	"When you're quiet or angry, I feel like you're withdrawing your love from me, and then I get afraid."
"You still haven't picked up my clothes at the dry cleaners?"	"When you don't do what I ask, I feel like you don't care about me."
"How many times have I talked to you about this?" (from boss at work)	"When you make the same mistake repeatedly, I'm afraid it will make me look bad. I hate it that you don't respect me. In the absence of Real Love, I really need respect. I also hate to bring up your mistakes over and over, because I'm afraid you won't like me when I nag you."

Notes

The Fourth Rule:

The next time you have a difficult conversation with some, remember to stop and think about what's happening. You're having trouble because one or both of you are not feeling loved. Until you address that problem, your conversation will not turn out as you'd like. If your interaction is going badly, tell your partner that you need to finish your conversation later, and then you can call or visit with someone who will unconditionally accept and love you. With that Real Love, you'll be able to go back to your original conversation much better prepared to listen and accept, which will make all the difference.

For an entire day, keep the four Rules of Seeing written on a three-by-five card in your pocket, and read them every hour. See what difference that makes in the conversations you have that day.

Pp. 103-111. Exercises in Truth-Telling

Do the exercises on these pages with a friend, or in a Loving Group. What matters most in these exercises is not getting an intellectual understanding of any given principle, but *feeling* unconditionally loved by other people as you share the truth about yourself.

Pp. 111-116. Giving Up the Getting and Protecting Behaviors

As we feel more unconditionally loved, we lose our *need* to use Getting and Protecting Behaviors, but we can also greatly accelerate our ability to feel Real Love if we make a conscious decision to give up the Getting and Protecting Behaviors which distract us. For the next seven days, make a commitment to give up one or two Getting and Protecting Behaviors (don't try to give them all up at once). When you do that, and as you also continue to tell the truth about yourself, you will feel increasingly loved. You could, for example, make a commitment to:

Notes

- absolutely refuse to continue any conversation where you feel angry (attacking). That's a big one.

- make no references whatever to what other people have done to you (acting like a victim).

- use no alcohol or drugs (running).

- not blame anyone else for how you're feeling (lying, attacking, acting like a victim).

- not put pressure on anyone to do anything for you (acting like a victim, clinging).

CHAPTER FIVE

The Effect of Real Love: Like Money In the Bank

Pp. 117-18. Real Love is Like Money in the Bank

Repeat the visualization on pp. 6-7 of *Real Love*. While you were feeling unconditionally loved by the people in the village, did you feel angry at them? Did you feel like using any other Getting and Protecting Behaviors with them? Of course not. More important, did you feel angry at *anyone else* while you were feeling loved—at your wife, husband, children, and so on?

Imagine carrying around with you the love you felt in the village—everywhere you go. Filled with that Real Love, you won't get angry at anyone. Now realize that you can find that kind of love in real life, just not in a mythical village in a visualization. As you feel the Real Love of friends, and as you remember that you have it, you will eliminate your emptiness, fear, and anger with *other people*—your wife, husband, children, boss, and others. This is a powerful concept.

Pp. 120-24. Healing Old Wounds with Real Love

Think about wounds from the past that are affecting your happiness:

- Parents who were not unconditionally loving (the most common wound of all).

Notes

- Sexual abuse.

- Verbal and emotional injuries.

- A marriage or engagement that failed.

Imagine how you would feel as you talked about these injuries with the people from the village on pp. 6-7 of *Real Love*. What you want most in life is Real Love—from any source—and as you get it, your wounds will heal. They won't matter anymore.

Talk about your past wounds with people who are capable of accepting and loving you. Don't just talk about your pain, however. Talk about the mistakes *you* have made. For example:

- Certainly the person (or people) who hurt you were unkind and unloving, but how were *you* demanding, controlling, and unloving in that relationship? (It is *not* appropriate, however, to talk about how you were wrong as a young child when other people treated you badly. Young children are not responsible to be loving when parents and others mistreat them.)

- Have you continued to nurse your anger at the people who hurt you? Have you used your anger to feel less helpless and alone?

- Have you used your past injuries to gain the sympathy of others (acting like a victim)?

- Have you exaggerated the part other people played in hurtful conflicts, minimizing the role you played (lying)?

You need to be accepted not just with your pain, but with your mistakes and flaws. As you share your failings, you'll find the healing power of Real Love.

Pp. 131-5. Gratitude

When people are not unconditionally loving toward us, the pain is often unbearable. It's natural that we remember those occasions more vividly than we do the few moments of Real Love we do experience with other people.

Think about times when people have seen your mistakes and flaws, and *not* been disappointed or angry at you. You may have had only a few of those moments—perhaps only recently as you've begun to tell the truth about yourself. It's critical to notice those times, to remember them, and to be grateful for them, because then you can store them up—put money in the bank—and achieve the happiness that comes from feeling sufficient Real Love.

Make a conscious decision in the next week to notice the kind things people say and do to you, and the times when they accept and love you with your flaws.

Notes

CHAPTER SIX

Sharing Your Fortune: The Power of Loving Others

Pp. 140-42. Learning to See Clearly

Imagine that you're starving to death—really starving, not just a bit hungry because it's been hours since you last ate—and into the room walks a man with a basket of food. What do you see? In that moment, your primary concern is the food in the basket, and you can see the man only as someone who will either give you some food or keep you from eating. You see him only as a potential source of food. You're too hungry to see him as someone who has his own needs and fears.

Now imagine a different scene. Again, a man walks into the room with a basket of food, but this time you've just eaten a full meal, and you have a limitless supply of food available to you. What do you see this time? Certainly you see the basket of food, but that's not your primary focus. Now you see that he's limping and grimacing as he walks, so you wonder if he's injured and might need your assistance. You also notice that he speaks with a heavy foreign accent, and seems to be lost, and you're filled with a desire to help him.

Actually, this is the same man who came in the room the first time, but on that occasion you didn't notice anything except the basket of food. You failed to notice who he was and what he needed because you were blinded by your own hunger.

Notes

Finally, imagine someone in your life who is a great source of disappointment or irritation to you. Consider the possibility that you see this person only in terms of what *you* need or fear. Blinded by emptiness and fear, you might be missing who he or she really is. Try to imagine what it would be like to be filled with Real Love—where you don't require anything from him or her, and you have no need to protect yourself—and make an attempt to see this person in a different way.

Pp. 142. Guilt

List some of the things you feel guilty about:

- A divorce. If only you'd been more understanding, or listened better, or been more loving, your marriage wouldn't have failed.

- Disappointing your family and friends. After losing your job and starting to drink, you've been wracked with guilt about letting everyone down.

- Your children are having lots of problems, and you know that you have a big role in causing them.

- You've said something unkind to a friend or family member, and since then your relationship has been cold and distant.

How has it worked for you to live with this continuous guilt? Has it led you to feel more loved, or to be more loving, or to be happier? If not, your guilt clearly *isn't working*, and you need to consider changing your attitude toward your mistakes.

A certain amount of guilt can be healthy, but only when it motivates you to avoid repeating the behaviors that detract from the happiness of yourself and others. Guilt that persists and doesn't contribute to feeling loved, loving, and happy is unproductive and must be abandoned. How can you lose that guilt?

Notes

Have you ever gotten up in the morning and thought, "You know, I'm feeling pretty loved and happy today. I *could* share that love with other people, but no, I think I'll keep it to myself instead. I'll be angry at people, and lie to them, and withdraw from them, just so I can cause them harm." Of course you haven't. Have you ever intentionally *decided* that you'll be hateful instead of loving? Ridiculous. Rather, you've been confronted with situations that required more love than you had, and then you've reacted selfishly to protect yourself or to get something for yourself.

Talk to a friend about a mistake you feel particularly guilty about. You might say, for example:

- "I (briefly describe what you did), and that was a real mistake on my part."

- "I have felt bad about that for months/years."

- "I am not making an excuse for what I did—it was wrong—but I'm beginning to see that with the skills I had at the time, and with my relative inability to be loving at the time, I couldn't have done a lot better than I did."

- "I need to talk about my mistake until I feel accepted enough by people like you that I don't need to feel guilty anymore. I only need to *see* my mistake and learn to avoid it better in the future."

Pp. 143-4. Accepting Other People

Think of a person (friend, family member, spouse) or group of people (fat people, foreigners, black people, white people, women, and so on) toward whom you have less than loving feelings.

Now think about *why* you have those feelings. We don't hate black people, for example, because of the color of their skin. We hate them because we have come to believe from past experience—or from what we've been taught—that they won't give us what we want, or they might hurt us in some way. We simply cannot accept

a person or group of people who refuse to fill our emptiness, or who might hurt us.

Imagine how your feelings toward that person or group would change if you had absolutely everything you wanted. If you didn't need anything from that person or group, and had nothing to fear from them, you could accept them for who they are, and your hatred would vanish. You'll have to repeat this exercise—and do what it takes to actually fill up with Real Love—many times before your old prejudices disappear.

Pp. 144-9. Telling the Truth About Whether We Accept Other People

There will always be occasions when people behave in ways that are inconvenient for us. We can't control that. We do have a choice, however, about how we *react* to people when they don't do what we want, and it's our reaction that reveals how we feel about them. When people behave in ways you don't like—when they fail to do as they've promised, when they inconvenience you, and so on—do you:

- Sigh with disappointment?

- Get a frown on your face?

- Speak in a stern tone of voice?

- Avoid the person who has behaved badly?

- Become demanding?

For the next week, closely observe yourself when people behave in ways you don't like. The *words* you speak aren't as important as all the body language, sighing, frowning, and other non-verbal forms of communication you use when you're disappointed or irritated. If you feel annoyed, you *will* communicate that.

Notes

When you're disappointed and annoyed, you're communicating that someone has done something to inconvenience *you*. You're concerned about something *you* didn't get, or about something that wasn't done for *you*. These are understandable feeling, but they're also selfish. You're telling other people that you care more about yourself than about them, and they can feel that every time.

When you realize how often you communicate disappointment and anger, talk about that with someone you know. Tell him or her how selfish you've been. Talk about how it has affected your relationships when you communicate with your irritation that you don't unconditionally care about the happiness of other people.

Pp. 147-8. Accepting Our Children

When your children make mistakes, inconvenience you, fail to do what you've asked, and make you look bad in public, what do you do? Do you:

- Sigh with exasperation?

- Raise your voice?

- Speak in a tone that says, "I mean business"?

- Move toward them in an aggressive posture?

- Use words that make them feel bad?

- Frown?

- Roll your eyes?

- Raise your hand?

If you're like virtually all parents, your answer to many of these questions is *yes*. Do children need to be corrected? Certainly, but what they need is information, guidance, and sometimes consequences

Notes

to *teach* them the best way to behave. When we're disappointed and angry at them, we're saying they have inconvenienced *us*, and that our primary concern in the moment is *ourselves*, not them. We're telling them we do not love them unconditionally, and that message cuts a child to the bone. There is nothing worse we could do, and when we communicate that message, they are wounded every single time. Feeling our disappointment and anger is so painful that they hear virtually nothing else we say.

For the next week, closely watch yourself in each interaction with your children. Do you show any of the signs above? Do you demonstrate disappointment and anger in any way? Nearly all of us do that as parents.

On the opposite page, write what you've learned about being a parent. You might write, for example:

- What my children need from me more than anything else is Real Love. They need to feel that I care about their happiness no matter what mistakes they make.

- When I'm disappointed and angry, I'm thinking of myself, not the love and happiness my children need.

- I have hurt my children on *many* occasions as I have failed to unconditionally love them. (List a few of those times.)

- I have always fooled myself into believing that I'm a great parent. I've always believed that I love my children.

- I hate to admit it, but with my disappointment and anger, I can see that I'm communicating that my love is conditional.

- I *am* loving my children the best I can—certainly as well as I was ever loved, or as well as I was ever taught by others—but it's not enough. Rather than defend what how I've taught them, I need to get enough Real Love in my own life that I can more easily love my children as they really need to be loved, and I need to make conscious decisions to be more loving.

Notes

- I will think about my being unloving every time I begin to feel disappointed or angry at my children.

- I will still have occasions when I'm not loving, but at least I will recognize them and admit them.

Talk to a friend about how you've been an unloving parent, and make a commitment to report to someone each time you're disappointed and angry at your kids. If you have this kind of accountability and truth-telling, you'll soon see just how selfish you've been, and you'll feel loved by people who accept you while you're selfish.

When you really get brave, sit down with your children and tell them how you've been selfish and angry, and how you're committed to learning how to be a better parent.

Pp. 149-51. Criticism

When your spouse, children, and others share with you the things they've done, or what they think, do you feel a compulsion to share with them your opinion about what they *should* have done, or what they should think?

- When people propose a plan of action, do you often have to offer a better way, without really stopping to listen and consider that their way *might* be just as good, only *different* from what you'd do?

- When people make mistakes, do you have to point them out every time?

- When people describe an event you witnessed, and they get some of the details wrong, do you jump in a correct them: "No, there were five people there, not four." Or, "That happened on Wednesday, not Thursday."

- Do you roll your eyes and get impatient when someone is speaking on a topic you think you know more about?

- Do you make "suggestions" about how people should dress, style their hair, prepare meals, and so on?

Unless you are quite unconditionally loving—and even sometimes when you *are* loving—your opinion, correction, or criticism will likely be received as unloving and hurtful. The next time someone shares an opinion with you, or tells you something he or she has done, just listen. You may have something brilliant to add, but just listen anyway and ask questions that serve only to get your partner to tell you more. Notice the reaction of your partner. Notice that he or she is more open and willing to tell you more.

Pp. 151-3. Apologies

When people offend you, do you expect them to apologize? Are you further offended when they don't? Do you require an apology before you'll forgive them? These are common attitudes.

Think of someone you believe owes you an apology. I recognize that he or she may actually have done something wrong, but when you demand an apology, you are saying the following:

- All people have the right to make their own choices in life—a world without that right would be intolerable but they lose that right when their choices inconvenience *me*.

- I am so important that when people make mistakes, they must express their regrets to me.

- I am so smart and pure that I have the ability to judge what people should or should not do.

- What I want is far more important than your happiness.

That's pretty heavy stuff to say to another person, but when you demand an apology, that is what you're saying.

Once you see the arrogance and lack of Real Love in your demanding an apology, go to the person you're thinking of and

apologize for your intolerance, anger, and lack of acceptance. You can briefly mention what that person did, but only so he or she knows what you've been unforgiving about. For example, you might say, "Last week/month/year, you (brief description of their transgression), and I've been holding that against you. I've been angry and critical, and that's wrong of me. I apologize." You will be astonished at the reactions you will get to your honesty and humility. Remember to keep your description of the other person's offense brief. Do not use this as an opportunity to remind him or her of what she did.

Pp. 154-7. Imposing Consequences

When other people do things that are wrong, or which consistently inconvenience you, you do have a right to speak up. Especially with children, you actually have a *responsibility* to correct behavior this is harmful to themselves and to others. Such correction must be delivered in a loving way, however, and if the person being corrected doesn't respond to loving guidance, consequences must sometimes be imposed.

Regrettably, most of us don't know how to impose consequences; we only know how to inflict punishment. What's the difference? Anger. Any consequence imposed while you're angry becomes a punishment, and it will teach people nothing except that you don't love them.

Think of the last several times you imposed a consequence on someone for behavior you didn't like. If you were irritated, you succeeded only in hurting someone. Talk about the times you've done that and admit the selfishness of your behavior.

Now, the next time you're about to impose a consequence, remember what you've learned, and it's unlikely that you'll repeat your actions.

Pp. 158-64. Loving Others

It would be so easy if all the people in our lives were unconditionally loving. Then we'd always be kind and loving toward them in return.

Notes

But if we're loving only toward those who are loving to us, that's not Real Love. It's unconditional love when we care about the happiness of others without their doing anything for us.

If you want a loving relationship with someone, the Real Love has to start somewhere—why not with you? As you make conscious decisions to behave in a loving way toward people, even when they are not loving in return, you will begin to supply the Real Love that other people need. You'll gradually remove their reason to use Getting and Protecting Behaviors, and you'll find your relationships becoming the loving experiences you've always wanted.

Choose someone with whom you are not having a loving relationship. Make a written commitment here that for the next several interactions you have with that person, you will not think about what you want from him or her. You will not protect yourself or insist on anything being your way. No matter what that person says, you will think about what could make him or her feel loved and happy. That does *not* mean you have to do whatever that person wants, but it does mean you will carefully listen and at the very least consider what would be in his or her best interest. The simple act of listening, not becoming angry, and not defending yourself will communicate love and acceptance.

If possible, make this commitment to a third party, to a wise man or woman, and then make a weekly report to that person about how you behaved relative to your commitment. If you failed to be loving, talk about that and create an opportunity to feel loved with your mistakes.

Notes

CHAPTER SEVEN

Playing a Beautiful Duet: The Joys of Mutually Loving Relationships

Pp. 170-73. A Mutually Loving Relationship

Imagine being in a relationship based on mutually shared Real Love. There will still be moments of disagreement, and even occasional disappointment, but the contention, anger, and manipulation we've come to accept as inevitable in relationships will be absent. A mutually loving relationship is the most fulfilling and precious experience in life.

As you picture this relationship, realize that it's only possible to have it if *you* are unconditionally loving. Two unhappy people do not add up to a loving relationship—that requires two people who are independently loved and loving. A beautiful duet really does require that you first be a competent soloist.

Write the following on the opposite blank page, and discuss it with a friend:

I will do whatever it takes to feel unconditionally loved, and to be unconditionally loving, even if the people around me don't do the same. I will take responsibility for feeling and sharing Real Love myself. My failures, my anger, and my unhappiness are my responsibility, not the fault of anyone else.

Notes

Pp. 170-73. Telling the Truth About Yourself to a Partner

Review the story of Harry and Elizabeth. Write the following on the opposite blank page, and discuss it with a wise friend:

"The next time my husband/wife/boss criticizes me for something I did wrong—or for something I didn't do—I will not defend myself. I will simply tell the truth about my mistake."

Think of a recent episode where someone pointed out a mistake you made—as Harry did with Elizabeth—and you defended yourself.

Write what you could have said instead of defending yourself. If you felt completely loved, and could be completely honest, what would you say about your mistake?

- You'd admit complete responsibility for your part of the mistake. You might say, for example, to your partner: "Yes, you're right. I didn't get that done on time, and I should have. I told you I would."

- You'd acknowledge the real reasons for your mistake, without excuses: "I didn't plan that well. I chose to do some other things, and my choices got in the way of doing what you wanted.

- You would not transfer the blame to others, even if other people did *contribute* to making the mistake. Other people may have slowed you up in the accomplishment of a task, for example, but they were not entirely responsible for the error. If you had adequately planned and followed up, the assignment would have been done on time.

Describe the above to a friend, and also talk about how you could have avoided the mistake.

If possible and appropriate, share what you've learned here with the person who originally pointed out your mistake. Say something like, "Remember when I didn't get home on time so you could use the car for an errand you had to do? And then I made some excuses about being late? I should just have told you it was my fault. I really could have made some choices differently and gotten home on time with the car for you. My mistake."

Afterward, talk to a wise friend about how it felt to tell the truth about yourself, and about the reaction of the person you told the truth to.

Pp. 173-5. Telling the Truth About Your Partner

Being human and fallible, the people around us make lots of mistakes. It is so easy to see them, and most of us have a strong tendency to point them out. Although we do sometimes tell people about their mistakes and flaws for *their* benefit, other motivations are usually involved:

- When we point out the mistakes of others, it makes us feel powerful and in control.

- When other people are making obvious mistakes, our own flaws look smaller by comparison.

- We sometimes like to bring up the flaws of other people simply to get revenge for the times they have pointed out *ours*.

When we remember that our primary purpose in life is to be genuinely happy—which is a result of feeling loved and loving others—our attitude toward describing the mistakes and flaws of other people changes considerably. When you get an urge to tell the truth about your partner, or to correct this person, consider the following criteria before you speak:

Notes

- Does it really matter? If your husband leaves the top off the mayonnaise jar only once in a great while, is this important enough to create the possibility that he might feel criticized if you point out this mistake? If someone at work brags about making fourteen sales that week, and you know it was really thirteen, is it really essential that you correct her?

- Can I be unconditionally loving when I say this? As you consider telling the truth about someone, are you free of disappointment and anger? If not, he will feel your selfishness, and you will not have a pleasant interaction. Go a step further and ask yourself, If I say this, and he defends himself, or otherwise doesn't accept what I'm saying, *then* will I feel disappointed or irritated? If so, do not speak to that person.

- Is the person I'm speaking to capable of hearing what I plan to say? If someone is sufficiently empty and afraid, she will not be able to hear you, even if you are unconditionally loving at the time. In most cases, it would then be unwise for you to speak. Talking to someone who cannot hear you is rarely productive.

Write down several instances where you did *not* follow these principles as you were speaking to someone about his or her faults. How did your conversation go? How did you feel? How did it affect your relationship with that person?

Write these criteria on a piece of paper or 3x5 card, and carry it with you for a week. Before you say anything to anyone about their behavior, read the card and think. Then describe to a friend how these principles changed what you said that week.

Pp. 177-84. Making Requests

You can't expect people to read your mind. If you want something, you need to ask for it. If you ignore the important principles below, however, making requests can be disastrous, leading to disappointment and conflict.

Notes

- Never forget the primary need for Real Love
- Make requests, not demands
- Make clear requests
- Don't push promises
- Never keep score

Never Forget the Primary Need for Real Love

Real Love isn't just one of the important things in life. It's always *the* essential ingredient in any productive interaction or relationship. When you make a request of someone, therefore, you must remember his or her need for Real Love. That need never goes away, and if you ignore it, you will not like the result of making your request, even when you get what you're asking for.

As you make a request, even though you're asking for something for yourself, you must remember the need of your partner to feel like you still care about him or her. The most important way to communicate love for your partner as you make a request is to make it without any trace of disappointment or anger. The words you choose, however, can also have an effect on how your request is perceived. Let's look at some examples of requests on the following page that are likely to be received badly, along with modifications of those requests to make them more palatable.

Notes

Request as We Often Make It	Genuine Request
Would you please stop leaving the milk out of the refrigerator?	When the milk gets left out, it spoils, and then I can't use it. Would you help me by putting it back in the fridge when you're finished with it?
Are you ever going to take the garbage out?	Mike, the garbage is getting pretty full. Can you take it out now?
We're late. Would you please hurry up?	It's important that we be on time to this. Can we start getting ready early so we're certain to leave in time to get there?

If your request includes any hint that the performance of your partner has been inadequate, your criticism is the only thing he or she will hear.

Make Requests, Not Demands

When you make genuine request of people, they can choose to freely give you what you've requested and get considerable enjoyment from their gift of time or effort. When you make demands, however, it takes all the fun out of it—for them and for you. When people don't give you what you demand, you feel disappointed and angry. Even when they do give you what you want, you only feel satisfied with fulfillment of your demand—as though they had filled an order you placed—rather than surprised, delighted, and loved. And it's not very fun for other people to simply fill your demands, which removes all the pleasure from what they give.

How can you tell the difference between a request and a demand? With requests, you don't feel disappointment and anger

Notes

when your request is denied. Write down or discuss with a friend or group some recent occasions when you became disappointed and irritated when you didn't get something you asked for. Admit that you weren't really *asking*; you were selfishly demanding that your needs be met.

Make Clear Requests

Read the story of Elizabeth and Henry on pp. 180-81 of *Real Love*. Have you ever been vague in making a request, and then been dissatisfied with the results because the person you asked didn't entirely understand what you wanted? Talk about such occasions. Following are some examples of vague requests that have been modified to be clearer.

Unclear Request	Clear, Productive Request
Can you help me sometime tomorrow?	Tomorrow morning I need to pick up some peat moss at the garden shop. Can you meet me in front of the house at nine o'clock with your truck so we can go together and get it?
You kids need to clean up the kitchen while I'm gone.	I'm leaving now and will be back home at nine-thirty. Will you two please wash the dishes, put away the food, and wipe off the counters by the time I get back?
Can we go out to eat sometime?	I'd love to go out and get something to eat. Can we go today at six-thirty?

Notes

Don't Push Promises

Once our partners have promised to do something, we sometimes treat them as though they're bound to us in chains. Yes, if your partner makes a promise, you do have a right to expect the promise to be kept, but if you push that right and become demanding, you'll destroy the Real Love in your relationship, and it's never worth it to do that.

Write down or discuss an occasion when you were irritated about your partner not doing something he or she promised to do. With that incident in mind, go through the following thought process:

- Everyone on the planet has the right to make his or her own choices. That is the Law of Choice. The world would be a miserable place without that right.

- We learn from making mistakes—they're essential to our growth—and people do not lose the right to make their own choices when they make mistakes, even when those mistakes inconvenience My Royal Highness.

- My partner—the person who has made me a promise is not an exception to the Law of Choice, even when I don't like his or her decisions.

- I can now choose to be angry and demanding—which will make both of us miserable—or I can make a loving choice: I can remind my partner of the promise that was made—without irritation—or I can just ignore the promise and decide what *I'll* do now that it hasn't been kept.

When you stop and rationally think like this, you won't keep injuring yourself, your partner, and your relationship with your disappointment, hurt feelings, righteous indignation, and demands.

Never Keep Score

Write or talk about the last several times you were irritated because your spouse or child or friend disappointed you. Almost invariably, we become annoyed with people only when we believe they *owe* us something, usually because we've done more for them than they've done for us. In other words, we have been *keeping score*, and we don't like it when other people get too far behind. Discuss what that attitude really means:

- If you're keeping score, that can only mean that the kind things you've done for that person were not unconditionally given. You were scoring points in order to obligate him or her to keep up with you—to do things for *you*.

- Keeping score is a completely selfish activity, designed only to get what you want for yourself. It's quite incompatible with Real Love.

- You've made it impossible for *you* to feel loved. You've created a situation where your partner feels obligated to struggle to catch up and even the score, and that will never feel like Real Love for you.

Discuss the selfishness of your keeping score, and resolve that you'll think of this the next time you're about to be irritated at someone for not doing what you want.

Pp. 184-6. Practicing Harmony

Describe a recent conflict between you and a partner. Your real goal—often forgotten in the heat of the moment—is to always play a loving, beautiful duet with each person in your life, and now you understand that the only way you can ensure accomplishment of that goal is to practice bringing the most loving individual instrument possible to the duet. With that in mind, how could you have contributed to harmony in your interaction, instead of

Notes

making the duet out of tune? What if you had offered to do more, instead of insisting on your partner doing more? What if you had admitted where you were wrong, instead of insisting on being right and pointing out your partner's mistakes?

Pp. 186-7. Faith in Mutual Love

One reason we keep score, and one enormous obstacle to a mutually loving relationship, is our belief that our partners are not doing all they can to contribute to the relationship. We note all our partners' failures and mistakes as proof that they're not trying and do not care about us. That will never change until we simply have faith that our partners are doing their best, despite their mistakes and flaws.

Think of a partner with whom you experience frustrations, and reconsider your relationship with him or her as you answer these questions:

- Are *you* not doing your best to be loving? Is there any time when you have a secret supply of Real Love that you simply refuse to share with others? Of course not.

- Do you honestly believe, then, that your *partner* has a secret supply of Real Love that he or she is refusing to share with you? Do you believe that your partner could choose to be a great deal more loving with you but simply withholds that love for the purpose of irritating you?

- Would you not feel much happier and more likely to be loving if you chose to have faith that your partner was doing her best?

- Would your partner not be happier and more likely to be loving if you had faith that she was doing the best she could?

- What do you really have to lose if you have faith in the intentions of your partner? Choosing to withhold that faith only guarantees distrust and unhappiness in your relationship.

Notes

CHAPTER EIGHT

Real Love in All Our Relationships: Spouses, Children, Friends, and Co-workers

Pp. 188-91. Marriage

So many people are frustrated with their spouses. 50-60% of marriages end in divorce, and lest we suppose that the remaining 40-50% live in a state of marital bliss, one study found that 45% of married women wish they could replace their present husbands. Our marriages are in a terrible state overall, and we need to understand *why*. Our present explanation—that there is something wrong with our spouses—is not giving us positive results.

Before you were married, how much consistent experience did you have with people who loved you? To answer that question, don't think about how people treated you when you did what they liked—when you were quiet, clean, helpful, grateful, cooperative, and otherwise convenient. It's no great trick for people to like you when you're being "good." The real question is, how did people treat you when you were foolish, weak, ungrateful, stupid, thoughtless, and when you otherwise failed to do what they wanted?

It's when you behaved badly that you learned how other people really felt about you. On those occasions, were they disappointed and irritated? Did they sigh, roll their eyes, and act exasperated and impatient? If so, you had the same *conditionally* "loving" experience most of us had, and it left you with a huge, painful hole in your soul.

Notes

When you married, then, you lacked the one thing—Real Love—that is most necessary to genuine happiness and healthy relationships. You were empty and hoped that your partner would fill you up and make you happy. In the beginning of the relationship, it probably even seemed like you were getting just what you wanted—you were in love with the way he or she made you feel—which is exactly why you married that person.

Think about the reasons you chose your spouse:

- She was so beautiful.

- He was handsome.

- She was bright and fun to be around.

- He was intelligent and responsible.

- She had a smile that lit up the room.

- He had a great job.

- She was nicer to you than anybody ever had been.

- He was flattering.

- He had a great sense of humor.

- The sex was fantastic.

In the absence of Real Love, all those characteristics became forms of Imitation Love that you hoped would make you happy. Then when the initial thrill wore off—as it always does—you were disappointed and bitter. You probably felt like your partner had let you down, perhaps even betrayed you.

Now that you understand the role of Real Love in all this, talk about the *real* reasons you're frustrated:

Notes

- Before you were married, you were already empty and afraid, which had nothing to do with your spouse.

- You expected that your partner would be able to make you happy, even though he or she didn't have the Real Love he needed either.

- You're disappointed and angry because he or she didn't fill *your* self-centered expectations for happiness.

- If you were unconditionally loving yourself, you'd be concerned about your partner's happiness, instead of making demands for yourself.

Once you understand the real problem, how can you keep being angry? How can you be angry at someone who is drowning? How can you expect him or her to save *you* from drowning?

Discuss what you've learned here with a friend. Finally, discuss what you've learned with your spouse. Admit to him or her that you've been selfish and demanding, and that you expected a miracle for yourself. This can go a long way toward healing a troubled marriage.

Pp. 191. Marriage Is a Commitment

Marriage is a commitment you make to stay with your partner while *you* learn to unconditionally love him or her. Are you willing to make that commitment? If so, you will learn a great deal about Real Love and have an excellent chance of creating a loving marriage. If, however, you insist on viewing marriage as an opportunity for you to get what you want, you will guarantee frustration and bitterness.

Make a written commitment that *you* will learn how to love your partner unconditionally. Review it every day. That commitment alone will change how you see many interactions with your spouse.

Notes

Share that commitment with a friend, and every week report on how you're doing with it.

Share that commitment with your spouse. Tell her that you've done a lousy job of loving her unconditionally, and tell her that you're going to do everything you can to learn how to be more loving.

Pp. 197. Exclusive relationships

If you're single, and if you've received insufficient Real Love in your life—which is the case with nearly all of us—you will have a natural tendency to look for someone to rescue you and supply you with the happiness you've always been missing. If you have those expectations—epidemic among those who are dating—you will ruin any relationship you have. You'll place impossible demands on your partner, and in the beginning you'll feel wonderful when you get all that Imitation Love. But then you'll eventually realize that no amount of praise, power, pleasure, and safety can make you happy, and you'll be enormously disappointed.

Avoid all that. Make this written commitment: "I will learn to tell the truth about myself and find people who can unconditionally love me. I will fill up with Real Love from friends—from people toward whom I feel no sexual attraction—until I feel the emptiness, fear, disappointment, and anger fade significantly from my life. Only when I feel enough Real Love—when I'm capable of really contributing to an unconditionally loving relationship—will I begin to look for an intimate partner.

This commitment will save you more heartache that you can possibly imagine.

Share this commitment with a friend.

Pp. 197-9. Sexual fidelity

Sexual infidelity is so destructive to marriages and other committed relationships that is must be avoided at all costs. What we often fail to realize, however, is that we can be unfaithful to our partners in many ways before we actually have sex with someone else. If

Notes

you want to avoid disaster in your marriage, you must make a commitment to avoid the following:

- Pornography. When you look at pornography, your sexual energy is not completely devoted to your spouse, and that *is* infidelity. In addition, it's quite naive to suppose that these thoughts wouldn't motivate you to some extent to find another sexual partner.

- Looking at other women or men in a sexual way. Men especially tend to look women over—mentally undressing them—as they see them in public. Although this may seem like an innocent activity, it's not. It's a diversion of your sexual loyalty to your spouse, and your spouse *will* notice this and be severely affected by your sexual wanderings.

- Having conversations with people that you wouldn't want your partner to know about. In any conversation with a person of the opposite sex, you need to ask yourself, Would I be willing to have this conversation videotaped for my wife to see? If not, you probably should be having it.

- Inappropriate touching and hugging. Would you touch or hug your brother or sister in the same way you're touching this woman?

- Sexual thoughts about people other than your spouse. Unfaithful behaviors are always preceded by unfaithful thoughts. Yes, I know that some thoughts simply appear out of nowhere, but it is always your choice whether you entertain and foster those thoughts. You can have all the sexual fantasies about your spouse that you want.

As you avoid the above activities, not only will you prevent damage to your relationship, but you will also avoid the serious distraction that these forms of imitation Love become in your search for Real Love.

Pp. 199-204. Sex

Sex is incredibly pleasurable, exactly why so many of us are obsessed with it: getting it, thinking about it, making ourselves sexually desirable, offering sex in exchange for other things we want, and so on. Think about the sexual pleasures you've enjoyed:

- The first time you had sex

- Looking at women as they walk by

- Pornography

- Masturbation

- Fantasizing about sex

How long did the pleasures of each of those experiences last? Not long, because almost immediately you were looking for the next source of excitement. And how many relationships have you maintained solely because they were sexually pleasurable? Not.

Sex is a wonderful addition to an unconditionally loving marriage. Outside that context, it almost always becomes a huge source of distraction and confusion, an opportunity to use our partner and ruin a potentially loving relationship.

I am *not* telling anyone here what they should accept as morally right. I *am* saying that people who are willing to make the following commitments are much more likely to find Real Love and an unconditionally loving partner.

- I will not have sex with a partner until I have first learned to tell the truth about myself, found Real Love from other people, and made a long-term commitment, i.e., marriage, with my sexual partner.

- I will stop entertaining the sexual thoughts I have toward anyone until I'm married to that person.

Notes

- I will not look at pornography of any kind, which means anything that provokes sexual thoughts.

- If I'm having sex with my present partner—to whom I am not married—I will stop, and I'll learn whether our relationship is based entirely on Real Love.

Pp. 206-12. Sex in Marriage

Sex can be used as a form of Imitation Love in marriage as well as outside marriage, and when we use it in that way, it causes harm to our marriages.

- Do you wish you had more sex than you do?

- Do you push your spouse to have sex with you?

- Are you irritated when your spouse doesn't want to have sex with you?

- Are you irritated when your spouse *does* want to have sex?

- Do you avoid having sex with your spouse?

If your answer is *yes* to any of these questions, you do not fully understand the healthy role of sex in marriage, and your attitude is hurting your relationship.

Write down how your demanding or resisting sex is hurting your relationship. For example, you might write:

- When I push my wife to have sex, I'm thinking about myself and not about her needs and fears. I am not being unconditionally loving.

- When I resist my husband about having sex, I am not thinking of his need to feel accepted by me. I'm protecting myself, which is understandable—who wants to have sex

with someone who doesn't care about you?—but I'm also causing harm to our relationship.

- My obsession with having more sex is a strong indication of my emptiness and fear. Although at this point I do want more sex, what I really need in my life is more Real Love.

- If I were unconditionally loving, I would want to contribute to my partner's happiness in any way I could. But I resist my husband about having sex, because I'm thinking about myself, not him.

- These arguments we have about sex are not making either of us happy, and I need to do something different.

Share your list with a friend.

Share your list with your spouse. If you're the partner who is more demanding about sex (in many cases, that is the woman), make a commitment to be more thoughtful of your partner and a great deal less insistent about what you want. If you're the partner who wants sex less, realize that offering sex—actually initiating it, rather than just giving in when the pressure is too uncomfortable—is a way of unconditionally caring about your partner, and will have a very positive effect on your relationship. Then offer sex as often as you are emotionally able—as a gift.

Pp. 212-16. Parenting

See earlier section in the *Companion*, which discussed pp. 147-8 of *Real Love*.

Pp. 219-21. Friends

Choose a friend you're feeling irritated at. Think about the real causes of your irritation: the lack of Real Love in *your* life, your emptiness, your expectations, and so on. Write out the conversation you're going to have with your friend. Among other things, you could say:

Notes

- I've been avoiding you lately.

- I've been irritated at you for a while. You could probably tell that.

- My being irritated is *not* your fault.

- I've been annoyed because you didn't do things *my* way, and that's been pretty selfish of me. It's embarrassing, really.

- I apologize for not being a good friend, for making demands instead of being interested in what you wanted.

Now have that conversation. Your friend is almost certain to respond well to your truth-telling. If he or she brings up even more things you've been selfish about, just acknowledge them. Tell the truth about your mistakes. Be free of the resentment, irritation, and demands that have been ruining your happiness.

Pp. 221-5. Strangers and People in the Workplace

Imagine someone cutting you off in traffic, or someone at work behaving in a way that makes your job difficult—late completing an assignment, requiring unnecessary work from you, and so on. When you get angry, consider what you are saying?

- I am the center of the universe. Everyone is obligated to run their lives with my convenience as their primary goal.

- I don't have to think about what would be convenient for everyone else, but they have to think about my wishes all the time.

- If I could, I would control other people like puppets or slaves.

- How dare you get in my way?

Notes

Our anger is selfish and arrogant, and it makes our happiness impossible. Describe to a friend some occasions when you have been angry at strangers or people at work. Realize and admit the selfishness of your behavior.

This does not mean, however, that you have to be a doormat for anyone who wants to use your or hurt you. On those occasions, you can always make choices that are not angry or defensive. Describe how you could have reacted in a loving way in each of the incidents you described earlier.

Pp. 225-6. God

Think of the times you have told the truth about yourself and felt moments of unconditional love from other people. Don't do this until you've actually exerted the faith to be truthful and have felt Real Love. Perhaps do the visualization again on pp. 6-7 of *Real Love*. Now imagine that feeling of love being doubled. Then tripled. Then multiplied a million times. That is the love God extends to you all the time.

With that feeling in your mind and heart, how does your relationship with God change? How does it change the way you pray?

CHAPTER NINE

Dealing with Obstacles on the Path to Real Love: Disappointment, Anger, and Getting and Protecting Behaviors

Pp. 227-43. The Elimination of Conflict

Conflict is utterly destructive to happiness and healthy relationships, and it must therefore be eliminated. You can do that as you remember the following principles:

- Realize that it's always about Real Love

- Listen (the four rules of seeing)

- Never speak in anger

- Tell the truth about yourself

- Tell the truth about your partner

- Recognize what you really want

- Determine *how* you and your partner can get what you want

Notes

- Remember the Law of Choice

- Refuse to be in conflict

Write these on a card and carry them with you. Memorize them, and use them whenever you sense the possibility of a conflict. Let's review them:

Realize That It's Always about Real Love

We can all give a million reasons for the conflicts we have, but they really boil down to one. Remember that conflict is disagreement accompanied by Getting and Protecting Behaviors, usually anger, and anger has one cause: an insufficient supply of Real Love. It really is that simple. Conflict isn't a result of poor communication, lack of commitment, or disagreements about money, sex, household duties, and children. Conflict occurs as people struggle over the scraps of Imitation Love that become so valuable in the absence of Real Love. When two people are starving to death, a crust of bread suddenly becomes very important, an object worth fighting about. In the presence of a mountain of food, however, the reason to fight simply disappears. Money, sex, household duties, and children are simply the *arenas* where we fight about the lack of Real Love and Imitation Love in our lives. Poor communication and lack of commitment are not the *cause* of conflict. Rather, they are *caused* by a lack of Real Love and always co-exist with conflict.

In short, conflict is always about Real Love—which isn't just *one* of the things we need to be happy; it's *the* thing we need—and until we see that, we can manage conflict, temporarily control it, and manipulate it to our advantage, but we can't eliminate it. If every time you see a conflict developing, you'll remember that you and the person you're talking to need to feel unconditionally accepted, you'll do much better with avoiding or eliminating the conflict.

Notes

Listen

Keep the Rules of Seeing, which we discussed earlier. Remember that when you genuinely listen to your partner, you communicate unconditional acceptance, which has more power to eliminate conflict than anything else.

Never Speak in Anger

We've learned that with anger, we feel stronger and less helpless, and we can often get people to do what we want, because anger provokes fear in the people around us. As Marcel Proust said, "To kindness, to knowledge, we make promises only; pain we obey." Our anger causes pain and fear in other people, and then they often leap to do whatever it takes to please us and eliminate our anger.

Because we've learned that anger can be quite effective, it's tempting to use it. But remember that what you get with any Getting Behavior is not Real Love, and you're also communicating to other people that you care about yourself, not them, which hurts your relationships.

With anger you may achieve some kind of strained agreement with people, but you will never truly resolve a conflict. When you're angry, therefore, use the five steps to eliminate anger, described on pp. 236-43 of *Real Love*.

Tell the Truth about Yourself

Most conflicts are characterized by multiple and often contradictory details that seem to weave an impossibly tangled web. Both you and your partner offer numerous and irrefutable proofs that you're right, and he or she is wrong. It can all be quite confusing.

How can you keep from falling into this awful web and making everything worse as you struggle with all the threads? The answer: Tell the truth about yourself—your emptiness and fear, your Getting and Protecting Behaviors, and your mistakes. Admit when you're wrong. Arguments tend to stop cold when you do this.

Notes

Tell the Truth about Your Partner

Everyone makes lots of mistakes, so it's easy to find fault with your partner. But it's rarely productive to focus on the mistakes themselves. What you need to see is that when people use Getting and Protecting Behaviors, they're drowning, and to save themselves, they're using the behaviors that often inconvenience and hurt other people—including you. When you understand that someone is drowning, how could you be hurt or angry? Who could be offended by the splashing of a drowning man? Or angry at him? But we do that all the time. We're actually irritated because our spouses are empty and afraid and are reaching out to save themselves with Getting and Protecting Behaviors.

Sometimes we do need to point out the actual mistakes of our partners—including their Getting and Protecting Behaviors—but that can only be done with Real Love.

Recognize What You Really Want

There once was a man who owned a beautiful apple tree. Although he enjoyed the delicious fruit he picked from it every day, he always wished he could reach the apples that were in the very top of the tree. One day, unable to resist his greed any longer, he cut the tree down and gorged himself on the fruit in the upper branches. Of course, he never again ate apples from the tree.

In every interaction you have with people, you're making a choice: You can enjoy the love and happiness available to you, or you can insist on more than you're offered—you can cut down the tree.

In every conversation, always ask yourself what you really want. Do you want to win this argument, *or* do you want to establish a long-term relationship that will benefit both of you? Do you want to be loving and happy, *or* right and miserable? Do you want to cut down the apple tree, *or* do you want to nourish it, prune it, and enjoy its fruit for a long time? Always remember that what you really want is to have the genuine happiness that comes from Real Love. Pay attention to that goal first and always, and then work on the other things you want.

Remember the Law of Choice

In every conflict, we're trying to control the choices of other people, and we do that only because we're afraid that otherwise we won't get anything we want. That's an illusion. You do not have the right to control the choices of other people, but that still leaves you with many choices of your own.

Determine *How* You and Your Partner Can Both Get What You Want

When we don't have enough of the Real Love we need more than anything else, we're painfully empty, and then it's natural that we feel like people should make us feel better by giving us exactly what we want. If they don't, we quickly find fault with them and conclude they don't care about us. When we're empty, we can be pretty demanding. From the time we were children, we were taught to identify and focus on the mistakes of others—after all, that was what people did with us. Teachers pointed out our errors on tests and essays. Parents pointed out when we *didn't* do what they wanted. In such an atmosphere of emptiness and fault-finding, reaching agreements is very difficult.

When people are not empty and afraid, however, and when they're not using Getting and Protecting Behaviors, most issues are fairly easy to work out. When you are determined to avoid a conflict, and to be concerned about the happiness of the person you're talking to, you will find a solution to the conflict that will please both of you. This is different than *compromising*, where you usually sacrifice something you want. In real conflict resolution, everyone is happy that the needs of everyone are being served best.

Refuse to Be in Conflict

The best way to respond to the Getting and Protecting Behaviors of your partner is to be unconditionally loving and use the principles we've discussed above. On some occasions, however, when your

partner pushes you to participate in an argument, you may sense that you're not capable of taking all the loving steps to eliminate the conflict. Perhaps you're running out of Real Love and sense that you're about to use your own Getting and Protecting Behaviors, which can only wound your relationship. Or you might see that your partner simply isn't in a condition to *feel* loved—no matter what you do—and is only intent on protecting himself.

When you see a potential conflict developing, however, you can always refuse to participate. Conflict is a choice. You can't determine the behavior of your spouse, but the two of you can't have a conflict without your participation. If you refuse to use Getting and Protecting Behaviors, your partner can still choose to be angry or otherwise manipulative, but the conflict will die for a lack of fuel from you.

Occasionally, your spouse might continue to attack you even though you refuse to participate in the conflict. Do not give in to your natural tendency to defend yourself. Make a conscious decision to physically remove yourself from the situation. This is quite different from the Protecting Behavior of running, because running is motivated by fear.

What exactly can you say when you want to withdraw?

- "My mistake." Admit you're wrong. When our partners are angry and criticizing us, we have a natural tendency to defend ourselves. As soon as you attempt to demonstrate that you're right, your partner will sense that you're also saying that he or she is *wrong*. People do not like to hear that they're wrong—because then they feel powerless and less lovable—so they naturally defend themselves from that accusation, direct or implied. You can defuse all that if you simply say, "My mistake." But what if you're certain you're right? Get over it. You can always find something you're wrong about. Perhaps you don't understand entirely what your partner is saying. Maybe you're foolishly defending the fact that you're *partly* right. And, of course, if you're irritated, you're wrong. If you have a need to be right, you will spark and perpetuate conflicts everywhere you go.

- "I'm not responding well to you right now, and that's not your fault. Let me collect my thoughts for a few moments and come up with a better way to address what you're saying."

- "I'm just not loving enough to continue this conversation. Can I come back to you in a few hours (or minutes, or the next day) and talk some more?"

When our partners argue with us, they have a goal. They want to feel safe, right, and in control. When we decide not to participate in a conflict, we're taking from our partners a morsel of the Imitation Love they want. For that reason, they might resist our withdrawal from the conflict that is feeding them in some way. You might have to repeat the above responses more than once. Sometimes you'll just have to say nothing at all. That might be uncomfortable at first, but eventually, if you refuse to be involved in the conflict, your partner will run out of steam. You might even have to leave the room, or the building.

Pp. 244-57. Dealing with Getting and Protecting Behaviors

Go through each of the stories on these pages and write a few words about similar interactions you've had. Write how you reacted, and how the conversation went from there. Then, with the understanding you have now of Real Love, write how you would like to react to such a situation in the future.

Share your observations with a friend or a Loving Group.

Pp. 257-68. Ending a Relationship

If you are contemplating a divorce, consider the following:

- Are you blaming your unhappiness on your partner, when the real cause is the inability you *both* have to feel and share Real Love?

Notes

- If you leave your marriage before you've learned how to find and share Real Love, you'll simply move on to another relationship that will be unloving and difficult—because you're the same unloving person as before.

- Are you willing to experience the profound rewards of keeping the commitment you made to stay with your partner and *learn* how to be loving?

Talk to a friend or group about what you realize as you consider the above questions.

If you have a friend who is contemplating a divorce, and who trusts your opinion, share with that person what you know about Real Love and suggest that he or she learn a lot more about loving before ending the relationship with his or her spouse.

If you are already divorced, look back at your marriage:

- Are you blaming your ex-spouse for your divorce, when the real cause was *your* inability to feel and share Real Love?

- Can you see your ex-spouse's behaviors—no matter how awful they became—as Getting and Protecting Behaviors, proving only that he or she was drowning?

- Understanding that your ex-spouse was drowning doing the best he or she could do—can you not easily let go of all the hurt and anger?

- Do you really want to spend the rest of your life angry at another person, creating only unhappiness for yourself?

CONCLUSION

Imagine that your best friend is moving to the other side of the world. You'll never see him or her again, so you decide to spend all the money you have—one thousand dollars—on a gift for your friend. Going to the largest department store in the area, you discover a huge variety of choices: clothing, jewelry, sporting equipment, music, electronic equipment, and so on. On one of the shelves you also find a bag of household garbage—waste paper, milk containers, old food, fruit peelings, and the like—and it's marked for sale at a thousand dollars.

Would it *ever* occur to you to buy the bag of garbage for your best friend, when for the same price you can get something much better? The question might seem ridiculous, but most of us make choices just that foolish. You have one life to live, and every day you make decisions about how to spend your limited time, talents, money, and physical and emotional effort. Surely you want to use your assets wisely, and purchase the greatest possible rewards:

- An inner peace that stays with you even when circumstances are difficult, even when the people around you are behaving badly

- A life without the pain of emptiness and fear

- An absence of the turmoil and anguish that always accompany disappointment and anger

- Deeply loving relationships

Notes

But most of us use our limited assets to buy garbage:

- Disappointment

- Anger

- Blaming and criticism

- Relationships filled with manipulation and contention

- Unfilled expectations

- The deadly unhappiness that always follows expectations, disappointment, blaming, and anger

If you're less than profoundly happy, if you're experiencing less than unconditionally loving relationships, you're spending everything you have on garbage. Do you really want to do that, when you could have infinite treasures instead? Never settle. Never be content to spend the assets of your life on Imitation Love, or Getting and Protecting Behaviors. Choose instead to be truthful about yourself, to feel the power of Real Love, and to share that love with those around you.

Resolve to take the steps necessary to feel and share Real Love. Read through the books, *Real Love* and *The Real Love Companion*, not once but over and over. As you dedicate yourself to living these principles, you *will* find the love and genuine happiness you've always wanted. I can make that promise with a certainty that comes from my own experience and from the experiences of thousands who have taken those steps.